Korean History Unveiled

A Journey Through the Centuries

Copyright © 2023 by Eun-ji Westwood and Einar Felix Hansen.

All rights reserved. No part of this book may be reproduced or transmitted in any form or by any means, electronic or mechanical, including photocopying, recording, or by any information storage and retrieval system, without written permission from the author, except for the inclusion of brief quotations in a review. This book was created with the help of Artificial Intelligence technology to assist in researching and organizing the information presented.

This book is intended for entertainment purposes only. While the author has made every effort to ensure the accuracy of the information presented, they do not guarantee or warrant the accuracy, completeness, or usefulness of any information contained in this book. The author accepts no responsibility or liability for any errors, omissions, or inaccuracies in this book, or for any actions taken based on the information contained herein. Readers are advised to consult with a professional for advice on any specific issues or concerns related to the content of this book.

The Geography and Early History of the Korean Peninsula 6

The Three Kingdoms Period (57 BCE-668 CE) 10

The Unified Silla Period (668-935 CE) 13

The Goryeo Dynasty (918-1392 CE) 16

The Joseon Dynasty (1392-1910 CE) 19

The Japanese Occupation (1910-1945) 22

The Division of Korea and the Korean War (1945-1953) 24

Reconstruction and the Miracle on the Han River (1953-1961) 26

The Park Chung-hee Era (1961-1979) 28

The Gwangju Uprising and the Democracy Movement (1980-1987) 30

The Roh Tae-woo and Kim Young-sam Presidencies (1987-1993) 32

The Kim Dae-jung Presidency and the Sunshine Policy (1993-2003) 34

The Roh Moo-hyun Presidency (2003-2008) 36

The Lee Myung-bak Presidency and the Global Financial Crisis (2008-2013) 38

The Park Geun-hye Presidency and the Sewol Ferry Disaster (2013-2017) 40

The Impeachment and Imprisonment of Park Geun-hye (2017) 42

The Moon Jae-in Presidency and the North Korean Nuclear Crisis (2017-present) 44

Religion and Culture in Korean History 46

Confucianism and Neo-Confucianism in Korean Thought 48

Korean Literature and the Korean Wave 50

Korean Art and Architecture 52

Korean Cuisine and Traditional Medicine 54

Education and Intellectual Life in Korea 56

Industrialization and Economic Development 58

Technology and Innovation in Korea 60

Labor and Social Welfare in Korea 62

The Korean Diaspora and Overseas Koreans 64

North-South Relations and Reunification 66

Korea's Place in the Global Community 68

Conclusion 70

The Geography and Early History of the Korean Peninsula

The Korean Peninsula is a land of rugged mountains, verdant forests, and stunning coastlines. It stretches for approximately 1,100 kilometers from north to south and covers an area of 223,697 square kilometers. It is located in Northeast Asia, bounded by the Sea of Japan to the east, the Yellow Sea to the west, and the Korea Strait to the south.

The peninsula has been inhabited by humans for tens of thousands of years. The earliest evidence of human habitation dates back to the Paleolithic era, around 500,000 years ago. Archaeological finds from this period include stone tools, animal bones, and fire pits.

As the millennia passed, various groups settled on the Korean Peninsula and established their own cultures. The first known kingdom on the peninsula was Gojoseon, which is said to have been founded in 2333 BCE by the legendary figure Dangun. According to myth, Dangun was the son of a god and a bear who was transformed into a woman. He is credited with introducing agriculture, hunting, and fishing to the Korean people.

The existence of Gojoseon is a matter of debate among historians, and there is limited archaeological evidence to support its existence. However, it is widely believed that the kingdom was located in the northern part of the peninsula, in what is now North Korea.

The Three Kingdoms Period (57 BCE-668 CE) marked the emergence of three powerful states on the Korean

Peninsula: Goguryeo, Baekje, and Silla. These kingdoms were frequently at war with each other, but they also engaged in cultural exchange, trade, and diplomacy.

Goguryeo was the largest and most powerful of the three kingdoms, and its territory encompassed parts of present-day North Korea, northeastern China, and Russia's Maritime Province. Baekje was located in the southwestern part of the peninsula, and its capital was located in present-day Seoul. Silla was located in the southeastern part of the peninsula and had a close relationship with the kingdom of Japan.

During the Three Kingdoms Period, the Korean Peninsula experienced significant cultural and technological advancements. Buddhism was introduced to Korea from China, and it quickly became a popular religion among the ruling elites and the common people. Art, literature, and architecture flourished, and the kingdoms developed their own unique styles and traditions.

In 668 CE, Silla defeated its rivals and established the Unified Silla Dynasty, which lasted until 935 CE. This period is known for its political stability, economic prosperity, and artistic achievements. Buddhism continued to be an influential force, and many of the country's most impressive works of art and architecture were produced during this time.

The Goryeo Dynasty (918-1392 CE) followed the fall of the Unified Silla, and it marked another golden age in Korean history. The dynasty was founded by King Taejo, who brought the various factions of the peninsula together under his rule. Goryeo is the origin of the English name "Korea."

Goryeo was influenced by both Chinese and Buddhist cultures. It established a civil service examination system based on the Chinese model, and it produced a number of influential Buddhist thinkers and scholars. The dynasty also experienced a renaissance in literature, and it produced some of the country's most enduring works of poetry and prose.

The Joseon Dynasty (1392-1910 CE) followed the fall of the Goryeo Dynasty, and it was the longest-lasting of Korea's dynastic periods. The dynasty was founded by King Taejo's grandson, Yi Seong-gye, who sought to establish a more centralized and Confucian-based government. Confucianism had become a dominant ideology in Korea during the Goryeo period, and it continued to play a significant role in the Joseon Dynasty.

During the early years of the Joseon Dynasty, the capital was located in Gaeseong, but it was later moved to Hanyang, which is present-day Seoul. The dynasty also made significant territorial gains, including the annexation of parts of Manchuria and the Korean ethnic region of Jeju Island.

The Joseon Dynasty was characterized by a rigid class system, with the ruling class, or yangban, enjoying significant privileges and status. Education was highly valued, and the civil service examination system was used to select officials based on their knowledge of Confucian principles and literature.

In the late 16th century, Korea faced a significant challenge from Japan. Toyotomi Hideyoshi, the powerful daimyo of Japan, launched two invasions of Korea in an attempt to conquer the peninsula and use it as a launching pad for further expansion into China. The invasions were ultimately repelled, thanks in part to the leadership of Admiral Yi Sun-sin and his famous "turtle ships."

The Joseon Dynasty continued until 1910, when it was annexed by Japan following the First Sino-Japanese War. The period of Japanese rule was marked by repression, forced labor, and cultural suppression. Many Koreans were forced to adopt Japanese names and were forbidden from speaking their own language or practicing their own customs.

Following World War II and Japan's surrender, the Korean Peninsula was divided into two zones of occupation: the north was occupied by Soviet forces, while the south was occupied by American forces. The division of Korea ultimately led to the Korean War, which lasted from 1950 to 1953 and resulted in the establishment of the Democratic People's Republic of Korea (North Korea) and the Republic of Korea (South Korea).

Today, South Korea is a vibrant democracy and one of the most prosperous and technologically advanced nations in the world. Its history is a rich tapestry of cultures, traditions, and struggles, and it continues to shape the country's identity and aspirations.

The Three Kingdoms Period (57 BCE-668 CE)

The Three Kingdoms Period is a fascinating era in Korean history that spanned over six centuries. It marked the emergence of three powerful states on the Korean Peninsula: Goguryeo, Baekje, and Silla. These kingdoms were frequently at war with each other, but they also engaged in cultural exchange, trade, and diplomacy.

The origins of the Three Kingdoms Period are shrouded in mystery, but it is believed to have begun in the first century BCE. The Han Dynasty of China exerted significant influence on the peninsula, and it is believed that the kingdom of Gojoseon, which had ruled over the peninsula for centuries, was replaced by smaller states that eventually coalesced into the three kingdoms.

Goguryeo was the largest and most powerful of the three kingdoms, and it had a territory that encompassed parts of present-day North Korea, northeastern China, and Russia's Maritime Province. Its capital was located in present-day Pyongyang, and it was ruled by a series of powerful monarchs, including King Gwanggaeto the Great, who expanded the kingdom's borders and established a powerful centralized government.

Baekje was located in the southwestern part of the peninsula, and its capital was located in present-day Seoul. It was known for its maritime culture and its close relationship with Japan. Baekje played a significant role in spreading Buddhism to Korea, and it was home to many of the country's most impressive works of art and architecture.

Silla was located in the southeastern part of the peninsula and had a close relationship with the kingdom of Japan. It was the smallest of the three kingdoms, but it had a strong military and a powerful aristocracy. Silla was also heavily influenced by Chinese culture and Confucianism.

The Three Kingdoms Period was characterized by frequent wars and political intrigue. The kingdoms often formed alliances and shifted allegiances in response to changing circumstances. In 372 CE, Goguryeo and Baekje formed an alliance to defeat Silla, but they were ultimately unsuccessful.

Despite their frequent conflicts, the kingdoms also engaged in cultural exchange and trade. Buddhism, which was introduced to Korea from China in the first century CE, played a significant role in shaping the culture of the period. Many of the country's most impressive works of art and architecture were produced during this time, including the Seokguram Grotto, a UNESCO World Heritage Site located in Gyeongju.

The Three Kingdoms Period also saw significant advancements in science, technology, and medicine. Goguryeo developed advanced metallurgy techniques, while Baekje was known for its shipbuilding and navigational skills. Silla developed a unique form of acupuncture that is still used today.

In the late sixth century, Silla began to emerge as a dominant power on the peninsula. It formed an alliance with the Tang Dynasty of China and launched a series of successful campaigns against Goguryeo and Baekje. In 668 CE, Silla defeated its rivals and established the Unified Silla Dynasty, which lasted until 935 CE.

The Three Kingdoms Period was a formative era in Korean history that laid the foundation for many of the cultural, political, and economic institutions that are still in place today. The kingdoms left behind a rich legacy of art, literature, and architecture, as well as significant advancements in science and medicine. The period also demonstrated the importance of alliances and diplomacy in maintaining stability and prosperity, lessons that continue to resonate in the modern era.

The Unified Silla Period (668-935 CE)

The Unified Silla Period was a time of political stability, economic prosperity, and artistic achievements on the Korean Peninsula. It followed the Three Kingdoms Period and lasted from 668 to 935 CE, during which the kingdom of Silla established its dominance over the entire peninsula.

The Unified Silla Dynasty was founded by King Munmu, who unified the Three Kingdoms and established a centralized government. The capital was located in Gyeongju, which is now a UNESCO World Heritage Site due to its many historical sites and cultural treasures.

During the early years of the Unified Silla Period, the kingdom faced significant challenges from its neighbors. The kingdom of Balhae, which had emerged from the remnants of Goguryeo, occupied territory in the northern part of the peninsula and frequently raided Silla's borders. The Tang Dynasty of China also posed a threat to Silla's sovereignty.

To counter these threats, Silla formed alliances with neighboring states and launched a series of military campaigns to expand its territory. Silla allied with Tang China and launched a joint campaign against Balhae, which resulted in the defeat of the northern kingdom and the annexation of its territory. The alliance with Tang China also helped to secure Silla's borders and establish diplomatic relations with other countries in the region.

The Unified Silla Period was marked by significant cultural achievements. Buddhism continued to be a dominant religion, and many of the country's most impressive works of art and architecture were produced during this time. The Seokguram Grotto and Bulguksa Temple, both located in Gyeongju, are considered to be among the finest examples of Buddhist art and architecture in East Asia.

The Unified Silla Period also saw significant advancements in science, technology, and medicine. The kingdom developed a unique form of acupuncture that is still used today, and it produced many talented scholars and scientists. The Hwarang, a group of elite warriors who were trained in martial arts and Confucian principles, were also established during this period.

The Unified Silla Period was also characterized by a rigid class system, with the aristocracy enjoying significant privileges and status. Education was highly valued, and the civil service examination system was used to select officials based on their knowledge of Confucian principles and literature.

The period was not without its challenges, however. The kingdom faced several rebellions and uprisings, including the Gyeon Hwon Rebellion and the Geomdeok Rebellion. These rebellions were often led by disgruntled aristocrats or regional leaders who sought to challenge Silla's centralized authority.

The Unified Silla Period ultimately came to an end in 935 CE, when a military general named Wang Geon established the Goryeo Dynasty. However, the legacy of the period continues to shape Korean culture and identity. The period laid the foundation for many of the cultural, political, and economic institutions that are still in place today. It also demonstrated the importance of diplomacy, military strength, and cultural exchange in maintaining stability and prosperity.

The Goryeo Dynasty (918-1392 CE)

The Goryeo Dynasty, which lasted from 918 to 1392 CE, was a formative era in Korean history that followed the fall of the Unified Silla Dynasty. The dynasty was founded by King Taejo, who brought the various factions of the peninsula together under his rule.

The Goryeo Dynasty was named after the ancient kingdom of Goguryeo, which had been one of the Three Kingdoms. The dynasty was characterized by a strong central government, a flourishing culture, and significant territorial gains.

The early years of the Goryeo Dynasty were marked by significant challenges. The Khitan Empire, a powerful state located in northeastern China, launched several invasions of the Korean Peninsula in an attempt to expand its territory. However, Goryeo was able to repel the Khitan invasions and establish itself as a dominant power in the region.

During the Goryeo Dynasty, the capital was located in Gaeseong, which is now located in North Korea. However, the capital was later moved to Hanyang, which is present-day Seoul. The dynasty was influenced by both Chinese and Buddhist cultures, and it produced a number of influential Buddhist thinkers and scholars.

The Goryeo Dynasty was also known for its literary achievements. It produced some of the country's most enduring works of poetry and prose, including the "Samguk Sagi," a history of the Three Kingdoms Period, and the

"Tripitaka Koreana," a collection of Buddhist scriptures that is considered to be one of the greatest achievements of East Asian printing technology.

The dynasty was also characterized by significant advancements in science and technology. Goryeo developed advanced metallurgy techniques, which allowed it to produce high-quality iron and steel. The dynasty also established a civil service examination system based on the Chinese model, which was used to select officials based on their knowledge of Confucian principles and literature.

During the late Goryeo period, the kingdom faced significant challenges from its neighbors. The Mongol Empire, which had conquered much of China, launched several invasions of the Korean Peninsula in an attempt to establish its dominance over the region. Goryeo was forced to pay tribute to the Mongols and suffered significant losses in territory and resources.

Despite these challenges, the Goryeo Dynasty continued to produce significant cultural achievements. Buddhism continued to be a dominant religion, and many of the country's most impressive works of art and architecture were produced during this time. The dynasty also saw significant advancements in medicine, including the development of acupuncture and moxibustion.

The Goryeo Dynasty ultimately came to an end in 1392 CE, when a general named Yi Seong-gye seized power and established the Joseon Dynasty. However, the legacy of the Goryeo Dynasty continues to shape Korean culture and identity. The dynasty laid the foundation for many of the cultural, political, and economic institutions that are still in place today. It also demonstrated the importance of diplomacy, military strength, and cultural exchange in maintaining stability and prosperity.

The Joseon Dynasty (1392-1910 CE)

The Joseon Dynasty, which lasted from 1392 to 1910 CE, was a transformative period in Korean history that followed the fall of the Goryeo Dynasty. The dynasty was founded by Yi Seong-gye, a general who had played a key role in the overthrow of the Goryeo Dynasty.

The Joseon Dynasty was characterized by a strong central government, a rigid class system, and a Confucian-based ideology. The dynasty was also known for its significant territorial gains, cultural achievements, and diplomatic relationships.

During the early years of the Joseon Dynasty, the capital was located in Gaeseong, but it was later moved to Hanyang, which is present-day Seoul. The dynasty was influenced by Confucianism, which emphasized the importance of education and the pursuit of moral excellence. The dynasty also developed a unique form of Neo-Confucianism that emphasized the role of the state in promoting social harmony and stability.

The Joseon Dynasty was marked by significant territorial gains. The dynasty annexed parts of Manchuria and the Korean ethnic region of Jeju Island. However, the dynasty also faced significant challenges from its neighbors. The Ming Dynasty of China frequently intervened in Korean affairs and attempted to establish its dominance over the peninsula.

During the Joseon Dynasty, Korea experienced significant cultural achievements. The dynasty produced some of the country's most enduring works of literature, including the "Annals of the Joseon Dynasty," a comprehensive history of the dynasty, and the "Jikji," a collection of Buddhist teachings that is considered to be the world's oldest extant book printed with movable metal type.

The dynasty was also known for its advancements in science and technology. The dynasty developed advanced agricultural techniques, which allowed it to produce high-quality crops and support a growing population. The dynasty also produced significant advancements in medicine, including the development of acupuncture and moxibustion.

The Joseon Dynasty was also characterized by a rigid class system, with the ruling class, or yangban, enjoying significant privileges and status. Education was highly valued, and the civil service examination system was used to select officials based on their knowledge of Confucian principles and literature. Women had limited opportunities for education and were expected to adhere to strict social norms.

In the late 16th century, Korea faced a significant challenge from Japan. Toyotomi Hideyoshi, the powerful daimyo of Japan, launched two invasions of Korea in an attempt to conquer the peninsula and use it as a launching pad for further expansion into China. The invasions were ultimately repelled, thanks in part to the leadership of Admiral Yi Sun-sin and his famous "turtle ships."

The Joseon Dynasty continued until 1910, when it was annexed by Japan following the First Sino-Japanese War. The period of Japanese rule was marked by repression, forced labor, and cultural suppression. Many Koreans were forced to adopt Japanese names and were forbidden from speaking their own language or practicing their own customs.

Despite its challenges, the Joseon Dynasty left behind a rich cultural legacy that continues to shape Korean culture and identity. The dynasty demonstrated the importance of education, diplomacy, and cultural exchange in maintaining stability and prosperity. It also produced significant advancements in science, technology, and medicine, and it laid the foundation for many of the cultural, political, and economic institutions that are still in place today.

The Japanese Occupation (1910-1945)

The Japanese Occupation of Korea, which lasted from 1910 to 1945, was a dark period in Korean history that followed the annexation of Korea by Japan. The occupation was marked by repression, forced labor, cultural suppression, and economic exploitation.

The annexation of Korea by Japan came at a time of rising nationalism and imperialism in East Asia. Japan had already annexed Taiwan and had defeated Russia in the Russo-Japanese War, establishing itself as a major power in the region. The annexation of Korea was seen as a way for Japan to expand its territory and resources.

During the early years of the occupation, Japan imposed a series of harsh measures on the Korean population. Korean names were banned, and the Japanese language was made the official language of the country. Koreans were also forced to adopt Japanese customs and dress, and they were forbidden from practicing their own religion or customs.

The Japanese also exploited the Korean economy, using it as a source of raw materials and labor. Many Koreans were forced to work in mines, factories, and on construction projects under brutal conditions. The Japanese also imposed heavy taxes on the Korean population and seized their land and property.

Despite these challenges, many Koreans resisted the Japanese occupation. Resistance movements emerged throughout the country, and there were several uprisings against Japanese rule. However, these movements were often brutally suppressed, and many Koreans were arrested, tortured, or executed for their involvement.

The occupation also had significant cultural impacts. The Japanese attempted to erase Korean culture and identity, destroying many historical sites and artifacts and suppressing Korean language and literature. However, many Koreans continued to practice their own customs and traditions in secret, and there were several significant cultural achievements during this time, including the development of Korean modern art and literature.

The occupation also had a significant impact on the political landscape of Korea. Many Koreans were inspired by the principles of democracy and human rights that were being promoted by the Allies during World War II. After Japan's surrender in 1945, Korea was liberated and the country was divided into two zones of occupation by the United States and the Soviet Union.

The Japanese Occupation was a dark period in Korean history, marked by repression, economic exploitation, and cultural suppression. However, it also demonstrated the resilience and determination of the Korean people in the face of adversity. The occupation left behind a legacy of cultural destruction and political turmoil, but it also laid the groundwork for the political and social movements that would eventually lead to Korea's emergence as a modern democratic state.

The Division of Korea and the Korean War (1945-1953)

The end of World War II and Japan's surrender in 1945 marked the beginning of a new chapter in Korean history. Korea was liberated from Japanese colonial rule, but it was immediately confronted with a new challenge: the division of the country and the outbreak of the Korean War.

After Japan's surrender, Korea was divided into two zones of occupation, with the Soviet Union occupying the northern half of the peninsula and the United States occupying the southern half. The division was meant to be temporary, but it quickly became clear that the two occupying powers had very different visions for the future of Korea.

In the North, the Soviet-backed Korean People's Army established a communist government under the leadership of Kim Il-sung. In the South, the United States established a democratic government under the leadership of Syngman Rhee. The two governments were unable to reconcile their differences, and tensions between North and South Korea began to escalate.

In June 1950, North Korea launched a surprise invasion of South Korea, sparking the Korean War. The war was fought between North and South Korea, with the support of their respective allies. The United States, Great Britain, and other United Nations countries supported South Korea, while the Soviet Union and China supported North Korea.

The Korean War was marked by significant violence and destruction. Both sides engaged in brutal tactics, including mass executions, bombings, and the use of chemical weapons. The war also had a significant impact on the civilian population, with many Koreans being displaced, injured, or killed.

The war lasted for three years and ended in a stalemate. A ceasefire agreement was signed in 1953, which established a demilitarized zone between North and South Korea. The two sides never signed a peace treaty, and the Korean Peninsula remains divided to this day.

The Korean War had significant political and social impacts on Korea. The war demonstrated the importance of international diplomacy and the need for a strong military defense. It also led to significant political and social changes in both North and South Korea. In the North, the war cemented Kim Il-sung's position as the country's leader and contributed to the country's isolation from the international community. In the South, the war led to the establishment of a strong military presence and contributed to the country's economic and political development.

Despite its challenges, the Korean War demonstrated the resilience and determination of the Korean people in the face of adversity. The war also highlighted the importance of international cooperation and the need for peaceful resolution of conflicts. While the Korean Peninsula remains divided, the legacy of the war continues to shape Korean culture and identity.

Reconstruction and the Miracle on the Han River (1953-1961)

After the Korean War ended in 1953, Korea was left devastated by the violence and destruction of the conflict. The country faced significant challenges in the post-war period, including rebuilding its infrastructure, reviving its economy, and establishing a stable political system.

The period of reconstruction following the Korean War is known as the Miracle on the Han River. The phrase refers to the rapid economic growth and modernization that took place in South Korea during the 1960s and 1970s, which transformed the country from a war-torn nation into a modern industrial powerhouse.

The Miracle on the Han River was made possible by a combination of factors. The government of South Korea, under the leadership of President Park Chung-hee, implemented a series of policies designed to promote economic growth and development. The policies included the establishment of export-oriented industries, the promotion of foreign investment, and the development of infrastructure such as roads, ports, and power plants.

The government also invested heavily in education and technology, creating a skilled workforce that could support the growth of the country's industrial sector. The country's geographical location, located between Japan and China, also played a significant role in its economic success, as it allowed Korea to become a hub for trade and investment.

During the period of reconstruction, South Korea's economy grew at an average rate of 8 percent per year, making it one of the fastest-growing economies in the world. The country's industrial sector expanded rapidly, with new industries such as electronics, steel, and shipbuilding emerging as major players in the global market. The success of the Miracle on the Han River was not without its challenges. The rapid economic growth and modernization led to significant social and cultural changes, with many traditional customs and practices being replaced by new forms of technology and consumer culture. The country also faced political instability, with the government of Park Chung-hee being accused of authoritarianism and corruption.

However, the period of reconstruction had a significant impact on the modern history of Korea. The Miracle on the Han River demonstrated the importance of government-led economic development and the potential for rapid growth and modernization in developing countries. It also established South Korea as a major player in the global economy, with the country becoming one of the wealthiest and most technologically advanced nations in the world.

Despite its success, the Miracle on the Han River also highlighted the importance of sustainable development and social welfare. The rapid growth and industrialization of the country came at a cost, with many Koreans suffering from the environmental, social, and economic consequences of the country's rapid modernization. Today, South Korea continues to face significant challenges in balancing economic growth with social and environmental concerns, but the legacy of the Miracle on the Han River continues to shape the country's identity and aspirations.

The Park Chung-hee Era (1961-1979)

The Park Chung-hee era, which lasted from 1961 to 1979, was a transformative period in Korean history that saw the country undergo significant economic growth and modernization. During this period, South Korea became one of the fastest-growing economies in the world, with a focus on export-oriented industrialization and government-led economic development.

Park Chung-hee rose to power in 1961 through a military coup, which ousted the democratic government of Prime Minister Chang Myon. Park Chung-hee established a new government that was focused on promoting economic growth and modernization, with an emphasis on export-oriented industries such as steel, shipbuilding, and electronics.

The government implemented a series of policies designed to promote economic growth and development, including the establishment of special economic zones, the promotion of foreign investment, and the development of infrastructure such as highways, ports, and airports. The government also invested heavily in education and technology, creating a skilled workforce that could support the growth of the country's industrial sector.

During the Park Chung-hee era, South Korea's economy grew at an average rate of 7 percent per year, making it one of the fastest-growing economies in the world. The country's industrial sector expanded rapidly, with new industries such as electronics, automobile manufacturing, and petrochemicals emerging as major players in the global market.

However, the Park Chung-hee era was also marked by political repression and human rights abuses. The government of Park Chung-hee was accused of authoritarianism and corruption, and there were frequent reports of torture and imprisonment of political dissidents.

The Park Chung-hee era came to an end in 1979, when Park was assassinated by his own intelligence chief. Despite its controversial legacy, the Park Chung-hee era played a significant role in shaping the modern history of Korea. The period of rapid economic growth and industrialization that took place during this time laid the foundation for South Korea's emergence as a major player in the global economy.

The Park Chung-hee era also demonstrated the potential for government-led economic development and the importance of strategic planning and investment in developing countries. However, the era also highlighted the importance of protecting human rights and ensuring a balance between economic growth and social welfare.

Today, South Korea continues to grapple with the legacy of the Park Chung-hee era. While the period was marked by significant economic growth and modernization, it was also characterized by political repression and human rights abuses. The legacy of the era continues to shape the political and social landscape of Korea, highlighting the ongoing tensions between economic development and democratic governance.

The Gwangju Uprising and the Democracy Movement (1980-1987)

The period between 1980 and 1987 was a time of significant political and social change in Korea. During this period, the country underwent a process of democratization, with a growing movement calling for greater political freedom and human rights.

The Gwangju Uprising, which took place in May 1980, was a turning point in this process of democratization. The uprising began as a protest against the military government of Chun Doo-hwan, which had seized power in a coup the previous year. The protesters were calling for greater political freedom and an end to government corruption and repression.

The protest quickly grew in size, and the military responded with force, using tanks and troops to suppress the protest. The violence that followed was brutal, with hundreds of people being killed and injured. The Gwangju Uprising became a symbol of the struggle for democracy in Korea, and it galvanized a growing movement of activists and intellectuals who were calling for political reform.

In the years that followed, the democracy movement continued to gain momentum. Activists organized protests, strikes, and rallies calling for greater political freedom and human rights. The movement was led by prominent figures such as Kim Dae-jung and Roh Tae-woo, who would later become president of South Korea.

The government responded with repression and violence, arresting and torturing political dissidents and cracking down on free speech and assembly. However, the democracy movement continued to grow, fueled by a growing sense of discontent with the government's repressive policies.

In 1987, the democracy movement achieved a significant victory with the adoption of a new constitution that provided for greater political freedom and human rights. The new constitution established a system of direct presidential elections, which paved the way for the election of Kim Dae-jung as president in 1997.

The Gwangju Uprising and the democracy movement of the 1980s were a pivotal period in Korean history. The struggle for democracy and human rights highlighted the importance of political freedom and the rule of law, and it demonstrated the power of grassroots movements in effecting change. The legacy of the democracy movement continues to shape the political and social landscape of Korea, highlighting the ongoing struggle for democracy and the need for ongoing vigilance to protect human rights and political freedom.

The Roh Tae-woo and Kim Young-sam Presidencies (1987-1993)

The Roh Tae-woo and Kim Young-sam presidencies, which spanned from 1987 to 1993, were a time of significant political and economic change in South Korea. The two presidents oversaw a period of rapid economic growth and modernization, as well as significant political reform and democratization.

Roh Tae-woo, who was elected president in 1988, inherited a country that was still grappling with the legacy of decades of military rule and political repression. Roh's presidency was marked by efforts to promote greater political freedom and democratic governance, as well as significant economic reforms aimed at modernizing the country's economy and making it more competitive in the global market.

One of the key reforms of Roh's presidency was the establishment of a system of direct presidential elections, which helped to solidify Korea's democratic institutions and ensure greater accountability and transparency in government. Roh also implemented significant economic reforms, including the privatization of state-owned enterprises and the liberalization of trade policies, which helped to modernize the Korean economy and make it more globally competitive.

Kim Young-sam, who succeeded Roh as president in 1993, continued many of the economic and political reforms initiated by his predecessor. Kim's presidency was marked by efforts to promote transparency and accountability in government, as well as significant social and environmental reforms aimed at addressing the country's growing wealth gap and environmental challenges.

One of the key reforms of Kim's presidency was the establishment of a new labor law that provided greater protections for workers and helped to improve labor relations in the country. Kim also implemented significant environmental reforms, including the establishment of a national park system and efforts to reduce pollution and protect endangered species.

The Roh Tae-woo and Kim Young-sam presidencies were a pivotal period in Korean history, characterized by significant political and economic changes that helped to modernize the country and establish it as a major player in the global economy. The legacy of these presidencies continues to shape the political and social landscape of Korea, highlighting the ongoing importance of democratic governance and economic development in promoting social and economic progress.

The Kim Dae-jung Presidency and the Sunshine Policy (1993-2003)

The presidency of Kim Dae-jung, which lasted from 1998 to 2003, was a time of significant change and reform in Korea. Kim Dae-jung was the first opposition politician to be elected president in South Korea, and his presidency was marked by a commitment to democratic governance, economic reform, and reconciliation with North Korea.

Kim's presidency was built on a platform of economic and political reform, aimed at promoting greater transparency and accountability in government, reducing corruption, and improving the quality of life for Koreans. One of the key reforms of Kim's presidency was the establishment of a new labor law that provided greater protections for workers and helped to improve labor relations in the country.

However, Kim's most significant legacy was his "Sunshine Policy," which aimed to promote reconciliation and cooperation with North Korea. The policy was based on the belief that greater engagement and cooperation between North and South Korea could lead to improved relations and ultimately to the reunification of the two Koreas.

Under the Sunshine Policy, South Korea implemented a range of initiatives aimed at promoting economic and cultural exchange with North Korea. These initiatives included humanitarian aid, joint economic projects, and family reunions for separated families.

The Sunshine Policy was not without controversy, with critics arguing that it was too conciliatory towards North

Korea and that it failed to address the country's human rights abuses and military aggression. However, the policy was widely popular in South Korea, and it helped to improve relations between the two Koreas.

Kim's presidency was also marked by significant social and environmental reforms, including efforts to address air and water pollution, protect endangered species, and promote renewable energy. Kim's commitment to environmental sustainability helped to establish South Korea as a leader in green technologies and renewable energy.

The Kim Dae-jung presidency was a pivotal period in Korean history, characterized by significant political, economic, and social change. The Sunshine Policy was a landmark initiative that helped to improve relations between North and South Korea, and it demonstrated the potential for peaceful resolution of conflicts and the importance of international diplomacy in promoting global peace and prosperity. Today, the legacy of Kim Dae-jung continues to inspire efforts towards reconciliation and cooperation between the two Koreas.

The Roh Moo-hyun Presidency (2003-2008)

The presidency of Roh Moo-hyun, which lasted from 2003 to 2008, was a time of significant political and social change in South Korea. Roh was the second opposition politician to be elected president in South Korea, and his presidency was marked by a commitment to social justice, economic reform, and transparency in government.

Roh's presidency was built on a platform of political and economic reform, aimed at promoting greater transparency and accountability in government, reducing corruption, and improving the quality of life for Koreans. One of the key reforms of Roh's presidency was the establishment of a new anti-corruption agency, which was aimed at rooting out corruption in government and promoting greater transparency and accountability.

Roh also implemented significant social and environmental reforms, including efforts to address air and water pollution, protect endangered species, and promote renewable energy. Roh's commitment to environmental sustainability helped to establish South Korea as a leader in green technologies and renewable energy.

One of the key challenges of Roh's presidency was dealing with North Korea, which was a significant source of tension and instability in the region. Roh continued the Sunshine Policy of his predecessor, Kim Dae-jung, and made efforts to promote engagement and cooperation with North Korea. However, the policy was criticized by some as being too conciliatory towards North Korea, and tensions between the two Koreas remained high.

Roh's presidency was also marked by efforts to promote social justice and equality in Korean society. Roh introduced policies aimed at reducing the wealth gap, including raising the minimum wage and expanding social welfare programs. He also made efforts to address the issue of low-paying jobs, which had become a significant source of economic and social inequality in Korea.

The legacy of Roh's presidency continues to shape the political and social landscape of Korea. His commitment to social justice and environmental sustainability helped to establish South Korea as a leader in these areas, while his efforts to promote transparency and accountability in government have contributed to the ongoing struggle for democratic governance in Korea. The challenges of dealing with North Korea remain a significant issue for Korea, highlighting the importance of ongoing efforts towards peace and reconciliation on the Korean peninsula.

The Lee Myung-bak Presidency and the Global Financial Crisis (2008-2013)

The presidency of Lee Myung-bak, which lasted from 2008 to 2013, was a time of significant economic and political change in South Korea. Lee's presidency was marked by a commitment to economic growth and development, as well as efforts to promote greater transparency and accountability in government.

One of the key challenges facing Lee's presidency was the global financial crisis, which had a significant impact on the Korean economy. The crisis, which began in 2008, was the worst economic downturn since the Great Depression, and it had a significant impact on countries around the world, including Korea.

In response to the crisis, Lee implemented a series of policies aimed at promoting economic growth and stability. These policies included stimulus measures aimed at boosting domestic demand, as well as measures aimed at stabilizing the financial sector and promoting trade and investment.

The government's response to the crisis was largely successful, and Korea emerged from the crisis in a relatively strong position. However, the crisis highlighted the vulnerability of Korea's export-oriented economy to external shocks and underscored the importance of promoting domestic demand and diversifying the economy.

In addition to the response to the financial crisis, Lee's presidency was marked by efforts to promote greater transparency and accountability in government. Lee introduced a range of measures aimed at reducing corruption and promoting greater accountability in government, including the establishment of a new anti-corruption agency and the introduction of new laws aimed at promoting transparency in government procurement.

Lee's presidency was also marked by efforts to promote social and environmental sustainability, including the introduction of new policies aimed at reducing carbon emissions and promoting renewable energy. Lee's commitment to sustainability helped to establish South Korea as a leader in environmental sustainability and green technologies.

The legacy of Lee's presidency continues to shape the political and social landscape of Korea. His commitment to economic growth and development helped to establish South Korea as a major player in the global economy, while his efforts to promote transparency and accountability in government have contributed to ongoing efforts to strengthen democratic governance in Korea. The challenges of promoting sustainability and addressing economic and social inequality remain ongoing issues for Korea, highlighting the importance of ongoing efforts towards progress and reform.

The Park Geun-hye Presidency and the Sewol Ferry Disaster (2013-2017)

The presidency of Park Geun-hye, which lasted from 2013 to 2017, was a time of significant political and social change in South Korea. Park was the first female president in South Korean history, and her presidency was marked by a commitment to economic growth and development, as well as efforts to promote greater transparency and accountability in government.

One of the key challenges facing Park's presidency was the Sewol Ferry Disaster, which occurred in April 2014. The ferry, which was carrying over 400 passengers, including many high school students, capsized and sank off the coast of South Korea. The disaster was one of the deadliest in Korean history, with over 300 people losing their lives.

The Sewol Ferry Disaster was a significant source of controversy and criticism for Park's presidency. The government's response to the disaster was widely criticized, with many accusing the government of being slow to respond and failing to take adequate measures to prevent the disaster.

The disaster also highlighted broader issues of safety and accountability in Korean society. The government's response to the disaster was seen as emblematic of a broader culture of corruption and lack of accountability in Korean society, which had become a significant source of public dissatisfaction and unrest.

Despite the challenges posed by the Sewol Ferry Disaster, Park's presidency was also marked by efforts to promote economic growth and development. Park introduced a range of policies aimed at promoting innovation and entrepreneurship, as well as measures aimed at boosting trade and investment.

Park's presidency was also marked by efforts to promote greater transparency and accountability in government. She introduced a range of measures aimed at reducing corruption and promoting greater accountability in government, including the establishment of a new anti-corruption agency and the introduction of new laws aimed at promoting transparency in government procurement.

The legacy of Park's presidency continues to shape the political and social landscape of Korea. The Sewol Ferry Disaster highlighted the ongoing challenges facing Korean society, including issues of safety, accountability, and corruption. However, Park's efforts to promote economic growth and development, as well as greater transparency and accountability in government, helped to establish South Korea as a major player in the global economy and contributed to ongoing efforts to strengthen democratic governance in Korea.

The Impeachment and Imprisonment of Park Geun-hye (2017)

The presidency of Park Geun-hye, which lasted from 2013 to 2017, came to an abrupt and ignominious end with her impeachment and subsequent imprisonment. Park's presidency had been marked by controversy and criticism, with her administration accused of corruption, lack of transparency, and authoritarianism.

In December 2016, a political scandal involving Park's confidante, Choi Soon-sil, came to light, revealing that Choi had used her connections to the president to influence government decisions and solicit bribes from large corporations. The scandal sparked widespread protests and public outcry, with many calling for Park's resignation or impeachment.

In March 2017, the Korean National Assembly voted to impeach Park, citing her involvement in the scandal and her failure to uphold the constitution. Park was subsequently stripped of her presidential powers and forced to leave the presidential palace.

Park's impeachment and subsequent imprisonment were a significant moment in Korean history, highlighting the ongoing struggle for democratic governance and accountability in Korean society. The impeachment process demonstrated the power of the Korean people to hold their leaders accountable for corruption and abuse of power, and it underscored the importance of transparency and accountability in government.

Park was later tried and convicted of a range of charges, including abuse of power, coercion, and bribery. She was sentenced to 25 years in prison, the longest sentence ever handed down to a former Korean president.

The legacy of Park's impeachment and imprisonment continues to shape the political and social landscape of Korea. The scandal and subsequent impeachment demonstrated the ongoing importance of promoting democratic governance and accountability in government, and it highlighted the ongoing challenges facing Korean society in addressing issues of corruption and abuse of power. However, the impeachment and conviction of Park also demonstrated the resilience of Korean democracy and the commitment of the Korean people to upholding the rule of law and democratic principles.

The Moon Jae-in Presidency and the North Korean Nuclear Crisis (2017-present)

The presidency of Moon Jae-in, which began in 2017, has been marked by significant efforts to address the ongoing North Korean nuclear crisis. Moon's presidency has been characterized by a commitment to diplomacy and engagement with North Korea, as well as efforts to promote domestic reform and address social and economic inequality in Korea.

The North Korean nuclear crisis has been a significant source of tension and instability in the region for decades, with North Korea's nuclear weapons program posing a significant threat to regional and global security. The crisis was exacerbated by the inflammatory rhetoric of former U.S. President Donald Trump, who engaged in a war of words with North Korean leader Kim Jong-un and threatened military action against the country.

In response to the crisis, Moon has pursued a policy of engagement and diplomacy with North Korea, aimed at promoting greater cooperation and reducing tensions on the Korean peninsula. Moon's efforts have included high-level talks with North Korean leaders, as well as efforts to promote economic and cultural exchange between the two Koreas.

While the North Korean nuclear crisis remains unresolved, Moon's efforts towards engagement and diplomacy have been widely praised, with many seeing them as a positive step towards resolving the crisis peacefully. Moon's approach has also helped to improve relations between South Korea and the United States, which had been strained by Trump's rhetoric and policies towards North Korea.

In addition to efforts towards resolving the North Korean nuclear crisis, Moon's presidency has been marked by efforts to promote social and economic reform in Korea. Moon has introduced a range of policies aimed at addressing economic and social inequality, including raising the minimum wage, expanding social welfare programs, and promoting greater gender equality.

Moon's presidency has also been marked by efforts to promote environmental sustainability and renewable energy, with Korea emerging as a leader in green technologies and renewable energy under his leadership.

The legacy of Moon's presidency will be shaped by ongoing efforts towards resolving the North Korean nuclear crisis, as well as his commitment to social and economic reform in Korea. The challenges of addressing the North Korean nuclear crisis remain ongoing, highlighting the importance of ongoing efforts towards diplomacy and engagement in promoting peace and stability on the Korean peninsula.

Religion and Culture in Korean History

Religion and culture have played a significant role in Korean history, shaping the beliefs, values, and traditions of Korean society. The history of Korean religion and culture is diverse and complex, with a range of influences from Buddhism, Confucianism, Taoism, Shamanism, Christianity, and more.

Buddhism was introduced to Korea in the 4th century CE, and it quickly became a dominant force in Korean religious and cultural life. Buddhism spread throughout the country, and many Buddhist temples and monasteries were established, many of which still exist today. Buddhism played a significant role in shaping Korean art, architecture, literature, and philosophy, and it remains an important part of Korean cultural heritage.

Confucianism was introduced to Korea in the 10th century CE, and it quickly became a dominant force in Korean political and social life. Confucianism emphasized the importance of moral and social order, and it became the basis for the Korean social hierarchy. Confucianism played a significant role in shaping Korean education, governance, and cultural norms, and it remains an important part of Korean cultural heritage.

Shamanism, also known as Muism, is a traditional Korean religion that has been practiced for thousands of years. Shamanism is centered on the belief in spirits and ancestors, and it involves a range of rituals and practices aimed at communicating with the spiritual world.

Shamanism played a significant role in shaping Korean folk culture, and it remains an important part of Korean cultural heritage.

Christianity was introduced to Korea in the late 19th century, and it quickly became a popular and influential religion in Korean society. Christianity played a significant role in the modernization of Korea, with many Christians involved in the independence movement and social reform. Today, Christianity is one of the most widely practiced religions in Korea, with over 30% of the population identifying as Christian.

Korean culture is also rich and diverse, encompassing a range of art, music, literature, cuisine, and more. Korean art is known for its vibrancy and beauty, with traditional forms such as pottery, calligraphy, and painting still popular today. Korean music is diverse, ranging from traditional folk music to modern K-pop, which has become a global phenomenon in recent years. Korean cuisine is renowned for its bold flavors and unique ingredients, with dishes such as kimchi, bibimbap, and bulgogi enjoyed around the world.

The legacy of Korean religion and culture continues to shape the social and cultural landscape of Korea today. Religion and culture remain important parts of Korean identity, with many Koreans embracing traditional beliefs and practices alongside modern values and traditions. The diversity and richness of Korean religion and culture are a testament to the enduring strength and resilience of Korean society.

Confucianism and Neo-Confucianism in Korean Thought

Confucianism and Neo-Confucianism have played a significant role in Korean thought and culture, shaping the beliefs, values, and social norms of Korean society. Confucianism was introduced to Korea in the 10th century CE, and it quickly became a dominant force in Korean political and social life. Neo-Confucianism, which emerged in the 14th century, built upon the principles of Confucianism, adding a greater emphasis on metaphysics and spiritual cultivation.

Confucianism emphasized the importance of moral and social order, and it became the basis for the Korean social hierarchy. Confucianism emphasized the importance of filial piety, respect for authority, and the cultivation of personal virtue. Confucianism also stressed the importance of education, with many Confucian scholars becoming influential advisors to Korean rulers.

Neo-Confucianism built upon the principles of Confucianism, adding a greater emphasis on metaphysics and spiritual cultivation. Neo-Confucianism emphasized the importance of self-cultivation and the cultivation of one's moral character. Neo-Confucianism also stressed the importance of the study of nature and the relationship between humanity and the cosmos.

Confucianism and Neo-Confucianism played a significant role in shaping Korean education and culture. Confucianism was the basis for the Korean education system, with many schools and universities following

Confucian principles. Confucianism also played a significant role in shaping Korean literature, art, and architecture, with many works of Korean art and literature reflecting Confucian ideals and values.

The influence of Confucianism and Neo-Confucianism continued to shape Korean society through the modern era. Confucian values and social norms played a significant role in shaping Korean attitudes towards family, gender, and social hierarchy. The influence of Confucianism also had a significant impact on the development of Korean democracy, with many Koreans embracing Confucian ideals of social responsibility and civic duty.

The legacy of Confucianism and Neo-Confucianism in Korean thought continues to shape the social and cultural landscape of Korea today. While the influence of Confucianism and Neo-Confucianism has waned in modern times, the principles and values of these philosophies continue to shape Korean culture and society. Confucianism and Neo-Confucianism remain an important part of Korean cultural heritage, and they continue to inspire ongoing efforts towards personal and social transformation in Korea.

Korean Literature and the Korean Wave

Korean literature and the Korean Wave, also known as Hallyu, have become significant cultural exports, spreading Korean culture and entertainment across the world. Korean literature is rich and diverse, encompassing a range of genres and styles, from traditional folk tales to modern novels and poetry. The Korean Wave, on the other hand, refers to the global popularity of Korean music, drama, film, and other entertainment.

Korean literature has a long and rich history, with many notable works dating back to the early days of the Three Kingdoms period. Korean literature includes a range of genres, including poetry, fiction, drama, and essays. Some of the most famous works of Korean literature include the Samguk Yusa, a collection of historical legends and folktales; the Tale of Chunhyang, a famous love story; and the works of Yi Sang, a modernist poet and writer.

In recent years, Korean literature has gained increased international recognition, with translations of Korean works becoming more widely available. Korean authors have also won several international literary awards, including the Man Booker International Prize and the Nobel Prize for Literature.

The Korean Wave, or Hallyu, refers to the global popularity of Korean culture and entertainment. The Korean Wave began in the 1990s with the spread of Korean popular music, or K-pop, and has since expanded to include Korean drama, film, fashion, and beauty. The Korean Wave has been credited with promoting Korean culture and tourism, as well as boosting the Korean economy.

Korean drama, or K-drama, has become particularly popular around the world, with many dramas gaining a dedicated following among fans. K-dramas often feature romantic storylines, as well as themes of family, friendship, and personal growth. Many K-dramas have become international hits, such as Descendants of the Sun and Crash Landing on You.

Korean literature and the Korean Wave have become significant cultural exports, helping to spread Korean culture and entertainment around the world. Korean literature reflects the rich cultural heritage of Korea, while the Korean Wave showcases the diversity and vibrancy of modern Korean entertainment. Together, these cultural exports have helped to elevate the profile of Korean culture on the global stage and promote greater cultural exchange and understanding.

Korean Art and Architecture

Korean art and architecture reflect the rich cultural heritage of Korea, with a range of styles and traditions that have evolved over centuries. Korean art and architecture are renowned for their beauty, elegance, and unique cultural identity.

Korean art encompasses a range of mediums, including painting, sculpture, pottery, calligraphy, and more. Traditional Korean painting often features natural landscapes, animals, and people, with bold brushstrokes and vibrant colors. Traditional Korean sculpture includes a range of styles, including stone, wood, and bronze sculpture, as well as intricate carvings and reliefs. Korean pottery is also highly regarded, with a long history dating back to the Neolithic period. Korean calligraphy is also an important art form, with a focus on the beauty and elegance of the written word.

Korean architecture is also renowned for its beauty and elegance, with a range of styles and traditions that have evolved over centuries. Traditional Korean architecture is characterized by its emphasis on harmony with nature, with many buildings featuring natural materials and elements such as wood, stone, and water. Traditional Korean architecture includes a range of styles, including palaces, temples, and houses. Many traditional Korean buildings feature sloping roofs and intricate decorative details, such as colorful roof tiles and ornate carvings.

Some of the most famous examples of Korean art and architecture include the Gyeongbokgung Palace, a royal palace built in the 14th century, and the Bulguksa Temple, a famous Buddhist temple built in the 8th century. Both of these landmarks are recognized as UNESCO World Heritage Sites, reflecting their significance and importance to Korean cultural heritage.

Korean art and architecture continue to evolve and thrive in modern times, with contemporary artists and architects exploring new styles and techniques. Korean contemporary art includes a range of mediums, from painting and sculpture to video art and installation art. Korean contemporary architecture also reflects a range of styles and influences, with many architects incorporating traditional Korean elements into modern buildings.

The legacy of Korean art and architecture continues to shape the cultural and artistic landscape of Korea today. Korean art and architecture are celebrated for their beauty, elegance, and unique cultural identity, reflecting the rich history and heritage of Korean culture.

Korean Cuisine and Traditional Medicine

Korean cuisine and traditional medicine reflect the unique cultural heritage of Korea, with a range of flavors, ingredients, and practices that have evolved over centuries. Korean cuisine is renowned for its bold flavors and unique ingredients, while traditional Korean medicine emphasizes the holistic approach to health and wellness.

Korean cuisine includes a range of dishes, from traditional staples such as kimchi, bibimbap, and bulgogi to modern fusion dishes that blend Korean and international flavors. Korean cuisine is characterized by its emphasis on fresh, locally sourced ingredients, with many dishes featuring vegetables, seafood, and meats. Korean cuisine also features a range of spices and sauces, including gochujang, a spicy red pepper paste, and doenjang, a fermented soybean paste.

One of the most famous and beloved Korean dishes is kimchi, a spicy fermented vegetable dish that is a staple in Korean cuisine. Kimchi is made from a variety of vegetables, including cabbage, radish, and cucumber, and it is often served as a side dish with rice and other Korean dishes. Kimchi is also considered to be a healthy food, with many health benefits attributed to its probiotic properties.

Traditional Korean medicine, or hanbang, emphasizes the holistic approach to health and wellness, treating the body, mind, and spirit as a whole. Traditional Korean medicine includes a range of practices, including herbal medicine, acupuncture, and moxibustion. Traditional Korean medicine also emphasizes the importance of maintaining balance and harmony in the body, with many treatments aimed at restoring balance and promoting overall wellness.

Many of the ingredients used in Korean cuisine, such as ginseng, ginger, and garlic, are also used in traditional Korean medicine, highlighting the close relationship between Korean cuisine and traditional medicine. Many Koreans believe that the foods they eat can have a significant impact on their health and wellbeing, and traditional Korean medicine plays an important role in promoting healthy eating and lifestyle habits.

The legacy of Korean cuisine and traditional medicine continues to shape the cultural and culinary landscape of Korea today. Korean cuisine has become increasingly popular around the world, with many Korean dishes gaining a dedicated following among food lovers. Traditional Korean medicine also continues to thrive, with many Koreans embracing its holistic approach to health and wellness. Together, Korean cuisine and traditional medicine reflect the unique cultural heritage of Korea, promoting healthy living and wellbeing for generations to come.

Education and Intellectual Life in Korea

Education and intellectual life have played a significant role in Korean history and culture, shaping the beliefs, values, and social norms of Korean society. Korean education has a long and rich history, dating back to the early days of Korean civilization. Korean education has evolved over time, reflecting the changing needs and priorities of Korean society.

Traditional Korean education emphasized the importance of Confucian values and social hierarchy, with many schools and universities following Confucian principles. Traditional Korean education was often reserved for the elite, with education seen as a pathway to social and economic advancement. Many scholars and intellectuals played an important role in Korean society, serving as advisors to Korean rulers and contributing to the cultural and intellectual life of Korea.

In modern times, Korean education has undergone significant changes, with the Korean education system becoming more inclusive and accessible to a wider range of students. Korean education is known for its emphasis on academic excellence and rigor, with many Korean students scoring highly on international tests of academic achievement. Korean universities are also known for their research and innovation, with many Korean universities ranking highly in global rankings.

Intellectual life in Korea has also thrived in modern times, with many Korean scholars and intellectuals contributing to the fields of science, technology, and culture. Korean intellectuals have made significant contributions to fields such as medicine, engineering, and computer science, with many Korean inventions and discoveries having a global impact.

The legacy of education and intellectual life in Korea continues to shape the cultural and intellectual landscape of Korea today. Korean education continues to emphasize the importance of academic excellence and achievement, with many Korean students pursuing advanced degrees in a range of fields. Intellectual life in Korea continues to thrive, with many Korean scholars and intellectuals contributing to global conversations and advancements in a range of fields.

Korean education and intellectual life reflect the unique cultural heritage of Korea, promoting the pursuit of knowledge, excellence, and innovation. These values continue to shape the social, cultural, and intellectual landscape of Korea today, contributing to the ongoing development and growth of Korean society.

Industrialization and Economic Development

Industrialization and economic development have been key drivers of growth and progress in Korea, transforming the country from an agricultural society to a modern, industrialized economy. Korean economic development has been characterized by a range of factors, including government intervention, technological innovation, and a strong work ethic.

Korean industrialization began in the 1960s, with the Korean government implementing a range of policies aimed at promoting economic growth and development. These policies included investment in infrastructure, education, and research and development, as well as support for key industries such as steel, shipbuilding, and electronics. Korean industrialization also benefited from a strong work ethic and a culture of hard work and perseverance.

Korean economic development continued to accelerate in the following decades, with Korean companies such as Samsung, LG, and Hyundai emerging as global leaders in a range of industries. Korean economic development was also supported by a range of government policies, including free trade agreements and investment in emerging industries such as biotechnology and renewable energy.

Korean economic development has had a significant impact on Korean society and culture, transforming Korea from an agricultural society to a modern, industrialized economy. Korean economic development has also led to significant improvements in living standards, with Koreans enjoying higher levels of income, education, and healthcare than in previous generations.

However, Korean economic development has also led to challenges and social changes, including income inequality, environmental degradation, and changes in social norms and values. Korean society continues to grapple with these challenges, seeking to balance the benefits of economic development with the need for social and environmental sustainability.

The legacy of industrialization and economic development continues to shape the economic and social landscape of Korea today. Korean companies continue to be global leaders in a range of industries, while Korean economic policies continue to prioritize innovation and growth. The ongoing development of the Korean economy reflects the ongoing commitment of Koreans to building a prosperous and sustainable future for their country and their people.

Technology and Innovation in Korea

Korea has emerged as a global leader in technology and innovation, with a range of companies and industries contributing to advancements in fields such as electronics, telecommunications, and biotechnology. Korean technology and innovation have been shaped by a range of factors, including government investment, a strong education system, and a culture of innovation and entrepreneurship.

Korean technology and innovation began to emerge in the 1970s and 1980s, with Korean companies such as Samsung and LG emerging as global leaders in the electronics industry. Korean technology and innovation were supported by government policies aimed at promoting research and development, as well as investment in emerging industries such as telecommunications and biotechnology.

Korean technology and innovation continued to accelerate in the following decades, with Korean companies contributing to global advancements in fields such as semiconductors, smartphones, and virtual reality. Korean technology and innovation were also supported by a strong education system, with many Koreans pursuing degrees in science, technology, engineering, and mathematics (STEM) fields.

Korean technology and innovation have had a significant impact on global culture and society, shaping the way people work, communicate, and live. Korean technology and innovation have also contributed to advancements in fields such as healthcare, energy, and transportation, with

Korean companies developing new technologies and solutions to address global challenges.

The legacy of Korean technology and innovation continues to shape the economic and social landscape of Korea today. Korean companies continue to be global leaders in a range of industries, with many investing in emerging technologies such as artificial intelligence and blockchain. The Korean government also continues to invest in research and development, seeking to promote innovation and growth in emerging industries.

Korean technology and innovation reflect the unique cultural heritage of Korea, promoting the pursuit of knowledge, excellence, and entrepreneurship. These values continue to shape the economic and social landscape of Korea today, contributing to the ongoing development and growth of Korean society.

Labor and Social Welfare in Korea

Labor and social welfare have been important issues in Korean society, reflecting the ongoing efforts to promote social justice and economic growth. Korean labor and social welfare policies have evolved over time, reflecting the changing needs and priorities of Korean society.

Korean labor laws have been shaped by a range of factors, including government policies, unionization, and globalization. Korean labor laws provide protections for workers, including minimum wage laws, maximum working hours, and workplace safety regulations. Korean labor laws also allow for collective bargaining and unionization, allowing workers to negotiate for better working conditions and pay.

Korean social welfare policies have also been shaped by a range of factors, including economic development, demographic changes, and government policies. Korean social welfare policies provide support for vulnerable populations, including the elderly, disabled, and low-income families. Korean social welfare policies include healthcare, pensions, and support for child care and education.

Despite these policies, challenges and inequalities persist in Korean labor and social welfare. Income inequality remains a significant issue in Korean society, with many Koreans struggling to make ends meet. The gender wage gap is also a significant issue, with women earning less than men for the same work.

Korean society continues to grapple with these challenges, seeking to promote social justice and economic growth. Recent government policies have focused on addressing these issues, including raising the minimum wage and expanding social welfare programs. The Korean government has also sought to promote flexible work arrangements and support for small and medium-sized enterprises, seeking to promote economic growth while protecting the rights of workers.

The legacy of labor and social welfare policies continues to shape the economic and social landscape of Korea today. Korean workers enjoy protections and benefits, while vulnerable populations receive support through social welfare programs. Korean society continues to seek ways to promote social justice and economic growth, seeking to build a prosperous and sustainable future for all Koreans.

The Korean Diaspora and Overseas Koreans

The Korean diaspora refers to the community of Koreans and people of Korean descent living outside of Korea. The Korean diaspora has a rich and complex history, reflecting the diverse experiences of Koreans living in different parts of the world. The Korean diaspora has played an important role in shaping the cultural and social landscape of Korea, as well as the countries in which they live.

The Korean diaspora began in the early 20th century, with Korean emigration to countries such as China, Japan, and the United States. Many Koreans left Korea in search of better economic opportunities or to escape political turmoil. Korean emigration continued to grow in the following decades, with Koreans settling in countries across the globe.

Korean overseas communities have played an important role in promoting Korean culture and identity. Korean overseas communities have established cultural centers, schools, and organizations aimed at preserving and promoting Korean language, culture, and traditions. Korean overseas communities have also been active in promoting Korean politics and social justice, advocating for issues such as reunification and human rights.

The Korean diaspora has also played an important role in economic development, with Korean overseas communities establishing businesses and contributing to the global economy. Korean overseas communities have been active in a range of industries, including technology, finance, and entertainment.

Despite the contributions of the Korean diaspora, challenges and inequalities persist in their experiences. Korean overseas communities face social and cultural barriers in adapting to their new countries, as well as economic and political challenges in maintaining ties with Korea. Korean overseas communities also face discrimination and marginalization, with many facing issues such as xenophobia and racism.

Korean society continues to grapple with these issues, seeking to promote social justice and inclusion for all Koreans, both in Korea and abroad. Recent government policies have focused on promoting stronger ties between Korea and the Korean diaspora, including support for cultural and economic exchange. Korean civil society has also been active in promoting the rights and welfare of the Korean diaspora, advocating for issues such as citizenship and political representation.

The legacy of the Korean diaspora continues to shape the cultural and social landscape of Korea and the countries in which they live. The Korean diaspora reflects the diversity and resilience of the Korean people, as well as their ongoing commitment to promoting social justice, cultural exchange, and economic development.

North-South Relations and Reunification

The division of Korea into North and South has been one of the most significant and enduring legacies of Korean history. The Korean War and subsequent decades of conflict and tension have shaped the economic, political, and social landscape of both North and South Korea. North-South relations and reunification have been important issues for both Koreas, reflecting the ongoing efforts to promote peace, reconciliation, and unity.

North-South relations have been marked by a range of factors, including political ideology, economic development, and international relations. The Korean War and subsequent decades of conflict and tension have made it difficult for the two Koreas to establish stable and peaceful relations. Both Koreas have taken different approaches to addressing these issues, with North Korea emphasizing its ideology of self-reliance and South Korea promoting a policy of engagement and cooperation.

Recent years have seen some positive developments in North-South relations, including high-level diplomatic meetings and the historic meeting between North Korean leader Kim Jong-un and South Korean President Moon Jae-in. However, challenges and obstacles persist in promoting sustainable and lasting peace on the Korean peninsula. Issues such as North Korea's nuclear program and human rights abuses continue to be significant obstacles to progress.

Reunification has been an important goal for both Koreas, reflecting the desire to overcome the legacy of division and promote unity and prosperity for all Koreans. Reunification could potentially bring significant economic, social, and cultural benefits to both Koreas, as well as promote peace and stability in the region. However, reunification also presents significant challenges, including economic disparities, cultural differences, and political issues.

Efforts to promote reunification have included a range of strategies and policies, including diplomatic engagement, economic cooperation, and cultural exchange. The Korean government has also established institutions and organizations aimed at promoting reunification, including the Ministry of Unification and the National Unification Advisory Council. Civil society groups and organizations have also played an important role in promoting reunification, advocating for issues such as family reunions and human rights.

The legacy of division and conflict continues to shape the cultural, economic, and social landscape of Korea today. North-South relations and reunification remain important issues, reflecting the ongoing efforts to promote peace, reconciliation, and unity on the Korean peninsula. While challenges and obstacles persist, the ongoing efforts to address these issues reflect the resilience and determination of the Korean people to build a better future for all Koreans.

Korea's Place in the Global Community

Korea has played an important role in the global community, reflecting its unique cultural heritage, economic development, and political influence. Korea's place in the global community has evolved over time, reflecting the changing needs and priorities of Korean society.

Korea has been a significant player in global trade and economic development, with Korean companies and industries contributing to the global economy. Korean companies such as Samsung, LG, and Hyundai have become household names around the world, contributing to a range of industries such as technology, automotive, and consumer goods. Korea has also been an active participant in global trade, with Korea signing free trade agreements with a range of countries and regions.

Korean culture and media have also played an important role in promoting Korea's place in the global community. Korean entertainment, including K-pop music and Korean dramas, have become increasingly popular around the world, leading to a phenomenon known as the "Korean Wave" or "Hallyu". Korean food and fashion have also gained significant popularity around the world, reflecting the growing interest in Korean culture.

Korean politics and diplomacy have also been important factors in Korea's place in the global community. Korea has been an active participant in regional and international organizations, including the United Nations, ASEAN, and the G20. Korea has also been a participant in efforts to address global challenges such as climate change and nuclear non-proliferation.

Korea's place in the global community is also shaped by its relationships with other countries and regions. Korea has maintained close relationships with its neighbors in East Asia, including China and Japan, while also seeking to expand its influence in other parts of the world, including the Middle East and Africa. Korea has also maintained a close relationship with the United States, reflecting the ongoing alliance between the two countries.

The legacy of Korea's place in the global community continues to shape the cultural, economic, and political landscape of Korea today. Korea continues to seek ways to promote its unique cultural heritage, while also contributing to the global economy and addressing global challenges. Korea's ongoing engagement with the global community reflects the resilience and determination of the Korean people to build a better future for all Koreans, as well as for people around the world.

Conclusion

The history of Korea is a complex and fascinating story, reflecting the diverse experiences and perspectives of the Korean people over thousands of years. From the earliest days of the Three Kingdoms period to the modern era of globalization and technological advancement, Korea has undergone significant transformations and challenges, shaping the cultural, economic, and political landscape of Korea and the world.

Throughout its history, Korea has faced a range of challenges and obstacles, including foreign invasions, internal conflict, and social inequality. However, Korea has also demonstrated resilience and innovation, seeking ways to overcome these challenges and promote peace, progress, and prosperity for all Koreans.

The division of Korea into North and South remains one of the most significant and enduring legacies of Korean history. North-South relations and reunification have been important issues for both Koreas, reflecting the ongoing efforts to promote peace, reconciliation, and unity. The Korean diaspora and overseas Koreans have also played an important role in promoting Korean culture, identity, and economic development around the world.

Korea's place in the global community is shaped by its unique cultural heritage, economic development, and political influence. Korea has contributed to the global economy, promoted cultural exchange and cooperation, and engaged in efforts to address global challenges such as climate change and nuclear non-proliferation.

The history of Korea is an ongoing story, reflecting the ongoing efforts of the Korean people to shape their own destiny and build a better future for themselves and the world. While challenges and obstacles persist, the resilience, determination, and creativity of the Korean people offer hope and inspiration for the future. As Korea continues to evolve and transform, its legacy will continue to shape the cultural, economic, and political landscape of the world for generations to come.

Thank you for taking the time to read this book on the history of South Korea. We hope that it has been an informative and engaging journey through the rich and complex history of this fascinating country.

If you enjoyed reading this book, we would be grateful if you could take a moment to leave a positive review. Your feedback will help us to improve our work and reach a wider audience, allowing more people to learn about the history and culture of South Korea.

Once again, thank you for your interest in this book, and we hope that it has left you with a deeper understanding and appreciation of the remarkable story of South Korea.

Made in the USA
Columbia, SC
10 January 2025